GRIEF MINISTRY

by

Yvette J. Fleming

BK Royston Publishing
P. O. Box 4321
Jeffersonville, IN 47131
502-802-5385
http://www.bkroystonpublishing.com
bkroystonpublishing@gmail.com

© Copyright – 2017

All Rights Reserved. No part of this book may be reproduced, stored in a retrieval system, or transmitted by any means without the written permission of the author.

Cover Design: Bill Lacy

ISBN-13: 978-1-946111-19-7
ISBN-10: 1-946111-19-8

Printed in the United States of America

Dedication

This book is dedicated to the loving memory of Florence Valerie Holt, a loving and devoted Mother, Grandmother and Great-Grandmother. Memories shared, thoughts remembered and words that inspired.

Thank You

Serving my Heavenly Father and my Lord and Savior Jesus Christ First, always and forever.

Thank you to my Mother Mrs. F.V. Holt for lifelong memories. To my Big brothers for inspiring me.

My Kids, Tamaria and Chris as well as my GrandKids, Nau'Shay and Demetrius Jr. for love without limits.

To my Publisher Julia Royston, for helping me to put my thoughts on paper.

A very special Thank You to Dawniel Winningham if it had not been for your words of wisdom and encouragement this book would still be in my head.

Thank you to Chandra for giving me the push I needed to get this done.

Why I'm Writing This?

I'm writing this book, because I hope it helps at least One Person. September is usually a month of celebration for me; my Birthday month. This September; however took a turn, a turn I wasn't expecting. I lost my Mother 'Florence Valerie Lewis Holt,' the day before my 53rd Birthday. The God that I serve is a sovereign God, and he will not put more on You than you can bear. I believe that. I Trust My God. He has gotten me through these past few months. Without my Faith, I don't know how I would have made it through her Home Going Service. You've got to believe in a Higher Power. All of you aren't going to believe in Jesus, but you have to have a Power higher that you believe and put your trust in. Now something else that I've done, is visit my mother's gravesite often. I work for the Postal Service and have lunch with my Mom every day. I told her, "I'll come every day until I don't have to anymore." It's therapy for me. Writing this book is also therapy for me. If you don't feel as if you can write a book, find a therapist or a community group specific to 'Grief.' Whether you're grieving a Parent, Sibling or someone who left the relationship; even a pet. Grieving a pet is very real. I have been there myself, in so much that friends thought a loved one (person) had passed. Grief is very real. And whether you're going through it now, have gone through it or know someone who is going through right now, you must know the importance of getting through it. I won't say 'get over it,' but 'you have got to get through it.'

TABLE OF CONTENTS

Introduction	
My Family	1
The Grandchildren's Perspective	9
My World Changed the Day She Passed	19
Days After the 9th of September	33
When the Calls Stop	37
The Clean Up	43
What Should the Family Do?	47
Coping with the Thought of	49
Conclusion	51
What To Do When A Loved One Dies A Survivor's Checklist.	55
Bible Verses To Help You Through	67

INTRODUCTION

I know that going through the grieving process is different for everyone. With the grieving process, I don't believe it's something you get over; it's something you get through. Recently I lost my Mother, who at the age of 89 died too soon, if you ask me. Having experienced grief up close and very personal, I want to help others with this process. Throughout this book, my prayer is that something that I say will be similar to an experience that you've had or may be experiencing right now that helps you through it. As stated before, it will be different for each person that reads this book. But in the end, my goal is to help, assist and support you throughout your grieving process.

Before I start with grieving, let me introduce you to me, my family and the one we all loved, cherished the most and thought was the best in the world: 'Our Mother.'

GRIEF

MINISTRY

My Family

I am the youngest of five children. I had four older brothers, but lost my youngest brother Tracy in April of 2005. I still think about him on a daily basis. He and I were the closest growing up together, living in the same house until his graduation from high school. My Mom always said she had two sets of kids. There is John Jr.: who now spells it Jon, who is 14 years older. Royce, who is 13 years older than me. Michael, who is 9 years older than me. Finally Tracy, who was 3 years older than me.

Hi, I'm Yvette the youngest, and my Mom's only daughter. Growing up in a single parent household, my Mom made it work. Having to feed 4 boys was a challenge, but she did it. Mostly on a large pot of pinto beans, rice and cornbread; She was a very strong woman. She grew up in Houston Texas in the Fifth Ward, and Graduated at the age of 16. In those days, schools only went to the eleventh grade. She went on to college in Louisiana, Xavier in New Orleans and Southern in Baton Rouge. She graduated with a BA of Science in Secondary Education in 1947. She married my Father in 1948, beginning her family in July of 1949 with the birth of John Jr. And one year to the date, my brother Royce was born. Don't ask me how she pulled that one off. My Mother continued her education, as she raised her family and taught Mathematics at her alma mater Phillis Wheatley high school, while receiving her Master of Science in Education from Texas Southern University in 1952. Two years later in November of 1954, Michael was born. In October 1960, along came her fourth child another boy 'Tracy.' On what she says was her last and final try for a girl in September of 1963, here I came. She figured I must've been a girl, with all the trouble I was giving her during birth. I was a breach baby; with the umbilical cord wrapped around my neck, we could have both died had the Doctor not gotten me out in time. But as you can see, we survived. I guess way back then, I must have known this world was crazy and wanted no part of it. My parents divorced when I was three months old, but my Mother had the help of both my Maternal and Paternal Grandmothers. 'It takes a village.' Mom continued to work for the school district; keeping those boys in line, and all the while spoiling me. Not rotten, but spoiled by Mom, my older brothers and Grandmothers. I still am; let some people tell it. Growing up in my house was adventurous to say the least; we had a lot of fun. I don't remember the year we moved into our house on Cosby Street in Houston's, what was then known as South Park. It was a big house from what I remember, but I was just a kid where everything was big. We had a den area where there was a pool table. I don't remember anyone playing pool, but I do remember letting the Guinea pigs run through the table, poking their heads in and out of the holes. We lived in a corner house next to a ditch. My brother Tracy and I would get bread and tie it to a string and catch crawfish. My mom would boil them for us; that was some good eating. I can remember my first experience with death. It was the death of our friend's Grandmother who lived on the other side of the street; she was called Little Momma. I can remember always going over and talking with her. About any and everything that a 5 year old could find to talk about, and she took the time to answer my questions out of love. I must have been about six maybe seven when she passed. When I found out, I cried and cried. I was sitting out on the front porch of our house crying, when my Mom brought me a popsicle and talked to me about death and heaven. My mom and I spent a lot of quality time together; leaving the boys and going to KIPS Big Boys; it was a burger joint. I would get a BLT with fries and a vanilla shake. I spent a lot of time at my Mom's mothers' house, because my Mom worked. I wasn't in school yet; or if I were in school, it was the summer time where one grand mother would take two of us and the other would have the other three.

　　We called my Mom's Mom 'Mother.' She was a school teacher from New Orleans. She moved to Houston after marrying my Grandfather who served in the military. My Mom used to tell me stories of the cow and chickens they had growing up, and her responsibilities of feeding the chickens. How when she would feed the baby chicks raw oatmeal, she would eat it with them. My Dad's Mother we called 'Dear.' 'Dear' was a beautician, who was born in a small town in Texas. I'm thankful that even though my parents were divorced, Mom allowed us to get to know 'Dear' and my cousins on my Dad's side. I'm grateful for time spent with both of my Grandmothers. I didn't know either of my Grandfathers; they both passed before I was born. Both of my Grandmothers taught me different things, seeing as how they both grew up in what almost seemed like different worlds. We lost both of my Grandmothers when I was in my twenties; they died a few years apart.

I think I get my strength from knowing how strong the women in my life were. My Mother was a single mother until I was nine when she remarried. By this time, my three oldest brothers were married with families of their own. It was just Tracy and I in the house, so we moved to an apartment in Humble Texas. Mom and her husband bought a house together where the four of us lived. Her husband Gene passed in 1980. His death was particularly hard on my brother Tracy, although Tracy had a relationship with our biological dad. Gene was there every day for us for eight years, and he helped my brother to grow. I had never seen my brother cry until the day we buried Gene. I think he lost a part of himself that day. I can't be sure, but I don't believe he allowed himself to grieve. He became a different person. It's my belief, 'That if you don't let it out, it will eat you up.' Yes, he cried, but he never spoke of that day ever again; never said how he felt. You've got to release some things that are inside of you, or you will become depressed or angry; possibly turning to drugs or alcohol to help alleviate the pain. You can't fill a void with something that is only going to make you feel empty. Tracy went on to college and eventually the Air Force, got married, had kids, got divorced and remarried until his death in 2005.

I got married, had two kids, got divorced and moved back home with Mom in 1986. Mom retired from HISD in 1987. She eventually moved out and got an apartment leaving me the house. She said, it was becoming too much of a responsibility for her. I think she just wanted some time to herself and figured I wasn't going anywhere any time soon, so she would move out. She moved two or three more times into apartments, before finally buying the house she lived in until her death.

Yvette J. Fleming

The Grandchildren's Perspective

Another reason I've written this book is for my children. To show the love they had for their Grandmother.

Our mother, my children's grandmother was so special. Here are some of the things that she did for them; she went above and beyond. I can remember when they were in grade school, how she would be the consummate educator that she was. She would have school with them in the summertime, so that they wouldn't forget the things they had learned the previous school year. So when school began again, they would have had a refresher course so to speak. She would also take them on field trips; different places like the zoo and museums. One year I went with them to Galveston for the butterfly exhibit, they had in Moody Gardens. Another trip we went on was to SeaWorld in San Antonio Texas. We had some interesting things to do in the summer time with the kids, and they never forgot the lessons that my mom taught them. You can see in the brief letters that they have written to her since her passing, what kind of effect she had on them. This lady! Yes, and I know that we are all born in sin and have all come short. I know my Mom wasn't a saint. But when I think back about my mother, I never heard her curse. I never heard her yell. If she would yell our names, it was because we were in a different room, and she wanted us to come where she was. You could talk to her about any and everything, and know that what you said was between the two of you. She never judged you. She wasn't a hard or very strict woman, but you knew when she meant business. These are just a few of the wonderful things about my mother. There are so many more things that I could tell but one book wouldn't be able to contain it all.

When she passed, she left behind four children (three boys and a girl), seventeen grandchildren, twenty-four great grands and one great-great grandson. She left behind a host of people, who love and miss her. And all of whom will grieve differently.

Here are two letters to her from my kids, who out of all her Grandkids were probably the closest to her. I say that, because they grew up with 'Mom.' After my divorce, we moved in with my mother for a while. The kids had to have been six and eight. So, she was there for them during their formative years. Being an Educator, my Mom would hold summer school with the kids; taking them on field trips, out for recess and the whole nine yards. When she moved out after about 4 years living with us, the kids had to re-adjust to her not being in the same space all the time. So, you can imagine the phone calls and visits. They missed her then, and they miss her now.

Yvette J. Fleming

From My Daughter

I wasn't going to say anything, but I decided to breathe. Today is the first day without my best friend. A person that would not judge me for what I wanted to do, was going to do and or did. I will never be able to replace my super spicy love bug. I loved you dearly. I wonder what you are doing, and who's with you. I won't kill any flies, because you'd always say: "I'd like to be a fly on the wall!" I'll just shoot them or tap them with a spray of Windex. Our relationship was one of a kind for 34 years (23 you know I'll always be 23). You have loved, taught, and showed me how to be strong. You adopted me as your own. When I'd watch those crazy judge shows, I'd fall sleep on your floor after being at work 12 hours and having to pick the kids up (when they move slow), you'd throw your crocheted blanket over me. Or when I'd sleep over, and you'd wake me up when I had 5 min before having to move! I will miss cooking for you, and telling you all the juicy stories in my day. No one will ever listen to me like you did. I am so jealous of those Angels that you get to walk with. I know I know. Why am I crying? You are waiting on me, and will be there when it's my time just like you were when you were here. I know you're laughing and thinking about that phone call, when I found my Pit Bull dead. This feeling is nothing like that one. I am at a loss for words and am probably rambling. I am not ok. I didn't lose you. You are with me always. I just have to leave a message after the beep, until you retrieve my messages from your new voicemail. You have taught me so much. And trust me, I heard everything you said. Thank youuuu sooo much for ALL you have done. ALL the knowledge you have shared and your kindness, it truly will be missed. To my best friend, I love you forever and always! REST IN PEACE FLORENCE VALERIE LEWIS HOLT! My days will never be the same. I will always hold you close to my heart! I am grateful to not have any regrets. I got to tell my grandma, I love her almost every day. Hug her at least 5 times a week, fuss with her 7 days a week and be at odds for about 30 secs a day (We both had to be right!). I will miss saying: "I knooowww mom," and her saying: "Ok Shay." Because Shay (my Granddaughter) says the same thing, but I really think she liked saying Cher like the New Orleans roots in her lol! It's hard to let go and not be able to see her again. Get on her nerves or just go over and sit next to her when I wanted to. So, I tell you all. If you are on my friends list, we have crossed paths somewhere down the line. I love ya. Good and bad, crazy or not, old or young, close or afar, you are in my heart! Mom showed me unconditional love as Jesus has, and I will no longer hold back from loving others as I have in the past. Janila Brown, thank you for the conference back in the summer time. I now see what the Pastor was telling me. I know I won't be able to speak at her funeral, so I'm getting my words out now!

It's strange! I guess I'm in denial, but it's like

you never left. I mean. I can't call for you to answer, but we talk every day. I can't see you and tell you how nuts my day is. And even with all of that.... I feel you aren't gone, but at peace. It's confusing yet peaceful. Very sad, yet I know I will see you again. If I've ever feared death before, I never will again, because I know I will see you again. I will still have bad days along with good days, but I won't have to wonder if you are with me, because I know you are. Rest in peace, till we meet again! Because, I am going to get on your nerves all over again. My love! Rip Mom!

Yvette J. Fleming

From My Son

It's been a 'lil over 2 months since you've been gone. There isn't one day I wish I had gotten to tell you how much you really meant to me. But my heart tells me, you already knew that. I never got to really grieve your death, and not sure when I will. But I do and for always will miss you. Since your death, as a person, I've changed and it may not be for the best. But from what I've heard, people are like trees. You have some leaves that may go one way or another. Or the limbs that may seem sturdy, but may not always support you. And also the roots that will always support you. You were definitely one of the roots that kept me whole and the sturdiest limbs ever known. Now that you are gone, I feel lost from time to time. I am very grateful to have my family and friends, there to support me thru all of this. I don't think people really appreciate those who support them until they are gone. But I will tell you this. Every single thing my grandmother did for me,

I do and will forever appreciate it. From telling me what I needed to do, to telling me how much she loved me. I didn't get the chance to tell her goodbye, but the last conversation we had I will never forget.. "Life is painful; always do right by them and yourself."

So as you can see, they both are grieving, but differently. The most important thing is that they are expressing their grief and seeking to move forward in spite of their pain. One day at a time.

My World Changed The Day She Passed

It was Friday September 9, 2016. I had just officially begun my vacation; the day before my 53rd birthday. The phone wakes me out of my sleep at eight o'clock that morning. My daughter was on the phone telling me she called the ambulance to come get Mom. That she may have been having a stroke. Now mind you; she woke me, so I was a little groggy, and she was nervous. So I asked her to repeat herself. Actually my words were: "wait what?" She repeated herself, and I told her I was on my way. I texted my 3 brothers to let them know what was going on. My oldest Jon was in Austin. Royce was in Colorado getting some mental rest; having just lost his wife Sharon in April of this year after a battle with cancer. Michael was on his way to Moms anyway to do some yard work. I hopped in the shower and hopped out. That had to be the quickest shower in history. Pulled my hair back into a pony tail and was out the door. My phone rang again; it was my daughter with the paramedics wanting to speak with me. I answered the questions. They told me Mom was having seizures. Seizures??? My Mom never suffered from seizures before, so in my mind I'm trying to figure out what in the world is going on. Let me take you back a couple of years. February of 2014, mom's alarm company calls me around 2:45pm saying her alarm had gone off and she wasn't answering the phone. They asked if I wanted them to call the police. I told them to give me a minute, let me call her because if may have been my grandkids going into the house. Mind you, my Mom is usually up and about early; showered, combed hair, has gone out to get the morning paper, fixed her coffee and morning news already turned on. When I call, she answers. I asked her a barrage of questions like: "Are you ok?"

"Yes," she says.

"Are you alone?"

"Yes."

"Is anyone with you?"

"No."

I asked her: "What happened? Why did the alarm go off?" I instantly become alarmed. Her answers were as if she were confused. She knew what she wanted to tell me, but couldn't get the words out. She would speak and it did not make sense to me. She would stop and say: "no I mean," or "umm." And she kept talking about the noise (The alarm siren). I told her I would be there as soon as I could. I hung up with her and headed back to the station. I'm a letter carrier for the USPS. As I got back to the station, I unloaded my truck (leaving everything at my case), gave my keys to my Supervisor and told her I had an emergency. I didn't wait for her response; I was out the door. Getting to Moms, I found her in her normal position sitting on the sofa knees up watching television. Her hair had not been combed, coffee hadn't been made and she hadn't eaten. We talk for a few minutes; I was still trying to make sense of the situation. She still couldn't tell me what happened. I asked her if she was hungry, and I fixed her something to eat. By this time, my daughter had gotten there. Mom was acting as if she had reverted back to a child when it came to eating, not knowing how to hold the spoon. I called my brothers, my Brother Royce's wife Sharon, who was a nurse. We started going through the symptoms and discussing what Mom could have had or may have had happen to her. They get there and decided Mom needed to go to the hospital. We go the emergency room and wait for hours. Finally going back to the back, the nurses are asking Mom questions. Things like: her name, birthdate, the day's date, the President of the United States. Things she would have normally known, she couldn't answer. Finally they admitted her, giving her fluids because she was dehydrated. My mom didn't like drinking water. Running a barrage of test from CT scans to MRI's; you name it, they ran it. Finding nothing except her magnesium being low, they add magnesium to her IV drip. She slowly but surely started coming around, answering the questions the nurses would ask. I asked her a question after we had been there for about eight hours: "Do you know my name now?" She looked at me as if I were losing my mind, and said "yes." I asked: "What is it?" She laughed, and said: "I thought you were kidding (she had to think for about a minute), then said: "Yvette." We both laughed; mine was a 'Thank God' relieve laugh. I stayed with my mom at her home for about a week; taking off work, leaving her only to go and check on my dogs and get fresh clothes. We had gone thru this one more time a year later. My daughter found her in her bedroom sitting on the floor. She called the ambulance, then me; again I text my brothers. Once at the hospital, they run the same test as the first time, finding nothing except dehydration. I told them the last time we were here that her magnesium was low. They run that test and add some magnesium to her IV drip. She gets better, but it takes a little longer this time. After a couple of days, she goes home. I stay with here for about a week; going to my house, looking after the dogs and then back to moms'. I stayed off work for about a week. After going back to work, I had a routine. I would leave Moms', go home check on the dogs, go to work, get off work, go home, check on the dogs, pack a bag and go back to moms'. This went on for an additional week, until she told me: "Go home, I'm fine." After this time in the hospital, my brother Michael told Mom: "We are not going to the hospital again for this same thing!" She agreed. Well this last time, it was definitely not the same thing. My daughter Tamaria called me while I was in route to the hospital, and told me she couldn't find moms wallet. I told her: "Go to the Hospital. You're overlooking it, because you're nervous. Just go to the hospital with mom. I'll stop by the house and look for it."

When I walked in the house, I just stopped and said: "Ok Mom, where is your wallet?" I looked in all the places she would normally have kept it; Nothing. "OK Mom, where is your purse?" I go into the bedroom, and her purse is on the bed. I look inside and find the wallet. When I get to the hospital, they tell me that there are already two people back there; My Brother Michael and my daughter. I called Mike to let him know I was there. He comes out, gives me his badge, and I go back to the ER not knowing what kind of condition I'll find my mom in. I have to pause right now. I'm tearing up from the memory of the day I last saw, spoke to and prayed over my Mother. When I walked into the room she was in, I was expecting to see her alert and talking, but that wasn't the case. I walked up to her, as she laid in that bed; IVs and EKG wires attached. I prayed she was resting comfortably. I sat down next to my daughter, we talked about how she found Mom, what the paramedics said and then we just sat. The nurse came in introduced herself, her name was Laurel. Mom hadn't had a seizure since the ambulance ride, but started having one about an hour after I got there. It wasn't what most people think (as seizures where the body is bucking out of control), hers was mostly the facial areas and her hand stiffening out and drooling out of control. I called the nurse who had just left to check on other patients. She comes in and does what they do. About 30 minutes later, she starts having another one. This time, the Doctor and nurses come in, work on her and get her stable. The last thing my Mom says to me is: "Please." She had to go to the restroom from all the fluids they were giving her. The nurses come in and tried to put her on a bedpan, but it hurt her. She said: "Pain." Taking her off, they placed an adult diaper on her, because she couldn't get up to go to the bathroom. Pain is the last words out of my Mother's mouth. Can you imagine how that makes me feel writing this to you; tears flowing as I write this out? Shortly after this, I asked Laurel if my brother could come back to the ER. She said: "Yes." After what seems like 10 minutes, he comes in. I give him verbal updates on mom. I had been texting him while he was in the hospital cafeteria, letting him know her seizures were coming more and more rapidly. I had texted all of my brothers updating them. My daughter left the room crying. Laurel asked me if she was ok, I told her that she and my Mother were very close and this wasn't easy for her to see. She came back in a few minutes later; as a different Doctor came in saying he was going to run some test on Mom to see why she was having seizures. He asked us: "If she were to code (cardiopulmonary arrest), do we want them to resuscitate her?" Of course! Our answer was: "Yes!" This was our Mother and Grandmother. I must tell you, I had to walk out of the room at this point. I walked around the corner, because I didn't want anyone to see me cry. But I just had a feeling, and it wasn't a good one. They asked us to go into the ER waiting room: a small room with about eight chairs a table with a lamp, two doors one to the outside lobby and one to the ER which was locked from the inside prohibiting you access to the ER unless someone on the outside opened it. We sat there for about 30 minutes, as they prepped mom for this procedure. Then they asked us to go up to the third floor where we could wait on her. About an hour later, they were asking us to go to the second floor where they would be doing the procedure. Before moving to the second floor, we heard them call a code blue in the ER. My daughter asked: "Do you think that was for mom?" I was sure it wasn't, so I told her I don't think so. They would have said something". While on the second floor, the Chaplain came and introduced herself (not a good sign in my mind). Moments later, the Dr. comes up and said; he didn't want to do the procedure because he felt she wouldn't survive it, so we could go back to the third floor and wait. My daughter asked him if that Code Blue was for my Mom; He said "Yes."

    We waited about ten minutes before going to the third floor. About thirty minutes later, the Nurse and Chaplain come in. The nurse asked, "if the Doctor had come to see us?"

    We said, "No."

    She said, 'she'd be right back.'

    I asked the Chaplain: "Is she gone?"

She says, "Wait on the Doctor."

She couldn't tell us anything until the Doctor came. Mom was gone; September 9, 2016 at the age of 89. My daughter asked the doctor if we could see her, we went to her room, tubes still in her mouth, we kiss her on the forehead, cried and tried to gather ourselves. The chaplain asks if she could pray with us, we said, "Yes." The prayer made me feel more at ease. I was able to use the phone app Glide to contact my son Chris who was in the military. I tell him to call me; not to glide me back. He calls about ten minutes later. I let him know Mom was gone. He cried; I tried to keep myself together for him; we hung up. Michael's wife Jean had come up to the third floor. I'm not sure how long she had been at the hospital. We hugged, and she gave us her condolences. My best friend Chandra had been calling throughout the day checking on Mom. She came up to the hospital, was in the parking lot wondering where to go and should she come up, because she hadn't heard from me in a while. She calls. I tell her we're on the third floor and that, "Mom was gone."

When she gets off the elevator, she sees us standing at the nurse's station. I'm filling out paperwork, and my daughter tells her not to give her a hug, because it's going to make her cry. Once I finish the paperwork, I give her a hug. We go to the waiting room to get Jean. Jean and Mike leave. I'm going to go to Moms' house because Tamaria's kids are there. They go there every day after school. Tamaria didn't feel as if she would be able to tell them Mom had passed, so, Chandra follows me to Moms house. While I'm driving, I'm singing, praying and crying.

"Lord, give me the strength to tell these two kids that their Great Grandmother was gone to heaven." We walk in; I sit the kids down and tell them mom had died. At the ages of eleven and twelve and having known Mom all of their lives, they handled it very well. They get their strength from Mom. Yes, they cried, but it wasn't uncontrollably. I tell them to get their things, so I can take them home. I turn on the alarm as we leave the house. Chandra goes her way, and I drive them home (going inside for a few minutes to make sure my daughter was ok). As I drove home, I thanked God for allowing me to have my mother for 52 years and 364 days.

Yvette J. Fleming

Days After The 9th Of September

Trying to figure out where to send your loved ones remains; well, is something to give a lot of thought too. I called friends and asked them to recommend Funeral homes. I went with the one most recommended. It was a family affair. Two of my brothers, my daughter and my oldest friend Angelia went to meet with the staff of the funeral home; this was on Tuesday. It was a warm welcome, and the director was very knowledgeable and supportive. He remembered all of our names by the time we left. There were caskets of different styles, colors and price ranges. And of course, the Guys left it up to me to choose the casket. But ultimately, Royce decided to go with an upgrade, which was alright with me. She wore Royal Purple and the casket was Lilac with Pink on the inside; it was lovely. We went back to the Funeral Home Friday for the formalities and to view Moms body. This was the first time Royce had seen her since her passing. Michael and I braced ourselves, because we had no idea what frame of mind Royce was really in. Remember, he had just memorialized his wife a few months earlier. But we all got through it just fine. The next time we would see each other, would be Monday, September 19, 2016. If you're wondering why it took from the 9th to the 19th, it's because: One, I was waiting on my son Chris to come back into the country. He's in the military and had just left in June. We were just making plans in the beginning of September for his return in December to celebrate Moms 90th Birthday. We hadn't anticipated his coming back this soon. We tried contacting the Red Cross to see if they could or would assist us in getting him home, but since she wasn't the person who raised him (but she did have an intricate hand in doing so), they couldn't help.

But needless to say, he got home. And Two, I was a bit selfish on my part. You see, my Step Father was in the Navy and was buried in The Veterans National Cemetery. They don't have services on the weekends, and I didn't want to go through or put my family through having her service on Saturday and waiting until Monday to bury her. I understand people do it, but I knew I wouldn't be in the right state of mind to handle that.

We decided the Limos would pick us up at my daughter's house. Once arriving at the church, we sat in the limos watching the people arrive, Once it got closer to service time, we exited the limos, went inside and viewed my Mother's body for the last time before the funeral officials lowered the lid. The Pastor preached, someone sang, people spoke very kind and loving words about my Mother and encouraging words to my family. Family, I hadn't seen in years were there. I believe that if I had not respected my mother as I did now and growing up, saying goodbye would have been a lot harder than it was. She raised us right. She had help along the way, in the form of my Grandmothers, my Step Dad and of course My Heavenly Father. She was a praying Mother and Grandmother, who stood a mere 5'4, thin frame all the years of my life. Who never had to raise her voice; you knew when she meant business. All four of her sons stood over six feet tall. The oldest John was the shortest of the four, he is 6'2. Royce 6'4, Michael 6'5 and her youngest son Tracy 6'6. And I stand at 5'6. I can remember mom and I overheard a conversation with two women who said, "How did that little lady have all those big boys?" Mom said to me, "It wasn't like they came here that size." We got a laugh out of that. She had a great sense of humor.

When The Calls Stop

After the immediate death of a loved one it seems as if the phone will never stop ringing. Texts keep coming and messages on social media are more and more prevalent. Friends, who normally wouldn't just stop by, do stop by, bringing food and encouragement. You always respond, "Oh, you didn't have to do that!" all the while thinking to yourself, 'Thank you, because I haven't had time to eat, let alone think about cooking.' Family, friends, co-workers and acquaintances make a point to keep in contact with you and make sure you've eaten. That you're moving around and not just lying in the bed moping. If you hadn't eaten, they make it a point to remind you to do so. And if you're lying around moping, you may get a surprise visit; especially from your best friend. But after the funeral service, the calls come farther and fewer in between. No one is stopping by checking on you as they once did.

Once you've gone back to work, co-workers smile or nod. Those who hadn't had the opportunity to call or text, give you their condolences and those too soon fade. So, what do you do now? Even though the calls from friends and family have slowed or stopped all together, don't you forget to call or text your immediate family; those family members who have lost Mom or Dad, Sister or Brother right- along with you. They still need the encouragement as do you. And if you're someone who prays, pray for your family. I've listed a few Scripture readings at the end of the book, if you need encouragement or need the words to encourage others. And remember, God gave us a few gifts. If He intended for us to not remember the ones we've lost, He wouldn't have given us memories. Cherish the memories. Write them down so that one day you can share them with your kids or grandkids maybe even your great grands. If you were lucky enough to have photos, put them in the cloud storage or on disks for safe keeping for sharing them as well. Make a video tribute of your loved one. Using a few of their favorite songs along with the pictures you have. A friend of one of my Nieces made a video for the family of my Mother; it was played at her funeral service. I also shared it on our family Facebook page and on my YouTube channel. These are just a few ways in which to keep the memory of your Beloved alive. I'm sure you can think of many more; put them into action, so future generations can get to know their family that has gone on.

But what will you do when the calls stop? Ask yourself that question. When you pick up the phone to call Mom, Dad, Sis, Bro, Husband or Wife (for a call you would ordinarily make), and it hits you that they're no longer there. What do you do when you need to talk? When you hear that song or see that movie that reminds you of them. Do you crawl up in a ball and go inside of yourself? Do you eat a half gallon of ice cream? "No, No You Don't." You find those memories and hold on to them. Whatever it was you needed to speak with them about, go ahead and ask them. You already know what they would have said. You can hear them in your head just as clearly; saying the words you know they would have spoken and then you smile.

Now, if you don't have anyone to talk to or you don't want to talk with anyone, WRITE! Write what you're feeling; good, bad, happy or sad, just WRITE. You've got to let it out one way or another. You've got to let it out or it will suffocate you from the inside.

You can't fill a void with things that are only going to make you empty, like drugs and alcohol or poisonous people. Sometimes people don't mean you the best, they don't have your best interest at heart. So I ask you to just rely on the Lord, and He will help you through this. He will guide you through this time. The person that has passed, take and keep them with you in your memories. Don't let the enemy tell you that you're nothing without them. Don't let the enemy fool you into thinking that the drugs and alcohol, the parties and late nights are going to fill that void. It won't. It makes it worse. So when I say to you: "WRITE your feelings down," it will help you to release everything that you've been holding on to. Create songs. Memories will stay with you for years. That: "I wish they can see me now, I wish they were here to see the grandchildren, I wish they were here, because I need so badly to talk with them;" though they aren't here physically, they are here with you spiritually. I know that you feel them, and you know they are around. You know what they would say to you, if they saw you filling that void with something that's going to harm you later. Write your feelings down; whether it's early in the morning or late at night and you can't sleep. Even if you have to get your baby's crayons and write on a napkin, I urge you to write your thoughts and feelings down. If you don't have anything to write with, speak into your phone; leave yourself messages until you can get somewhere to write your thoughts down. Your thoughts like mine, could lead you to write a book.

If you find yourself at a point where you really do need to speak with someone, go to Google to find Grief Counseling in your area. Or if your Job has EAP, contact them and make an appointment. Make it a point to do something and talk with someone. It could be a girlfriend, boyfriend, best friend, homeboy or someone. You must let it out! Don't let it suffocate you from the inside out.

This leads me to remind you. If you already know, just need to encourage yourself or if you don't know: Isaiah 9:6 New International Version (NIV)

6 "For to us a child is born, to us a son is given, and the government will be on his shoulders.

And he will be called Wonderful Counselor, Mighty God, Everlasting Father, and Prince of Peace."

We were given a Counselor from God. If you have trouble speaking with people, give Jesus a try.

The Clean Up

Mom had been in her house about twelve years, so you know she'd accumulated a lot of things. The clean-up has not been easy. To tell you the truth, it's December and it still isn't cleaned out, but we are working on it. Paperwork, furniture, turning off the cable; the small things, pictures, clothes, linens; throwing things out. What to keep, what to give to who and what to give to what charity. Did I mention the Paperwork? Then you have the sentimental things: mugs you bought for her on trips you went on, computers, laptops you'd given her; clocks. Boxing up the dishes and deciding what to do with the house. The house; even though I never lived there, had sentimental value to me as well. I stayed there for about four to five weeks after having surgery; went to stay some nights just because. Staying there after her hospital stays; saying to myself after this last time she was in the hospital,

"Ok, she is just going to have to come and stay with me once she gets out this time." You want your parents to have their independence, but at some point you have to say: 'No, not any more. You're coming home with me.' She took herself off driving, after getting lost while leaving a doctor's appointment a few years back. We put out a missing person's report, because my Mom didn't drive at night because of her cataracts. It was dusk, and she still wasn't home. Normally I wouldn't worry about her being out at dark, but since she stopped driving nights a few years before getting lost, we called the police for help. It's time for us to make a sacrifice like they did for you.

When you lose a loved you, there is always that, "What could I have done differently? If I had only said this or that, or I should have done more." STOP! Don't let that eat at you. We all go through it; no matter how much or little we actually did. It wasn't enough in our minds. So needless to say, cleaning the house has been a slow but sure process.

Cleaning the house, what to keep, what to throw away. Going through clothes, bills and personal things deciding who gets what? How do you decide? I have heard horror stories of families fighting even before the funeral. I refused to fight with my brothers, and I feel they felt the same way. So far things have gone smoothly. I've asked my brothers what they wanted, they picked, they got. Done! My brother Michael has been a champ through this process. He helped with moving and removing the large objects of furniture from the home, cleaning and making it ready to paint. There is still so much to go through; Mom had a lot of stuff. She didn't go out to shop much anymore, and she could shop in her day. But she still managed to shop online or through magazines. There are a lot of gifts to go through to try and figure out, who she wanted to give what to. That's the hard part. She didn't have many bills. No credit cards, no car note and very few medical bills. That part makes this process a little easier. If you're like me and this process becomes over whelming, get the important things out of the house. Documents; anything that is of legal content, things that you and your family want to keep, and hire a cleaning crew to come in and do the rest.

But what if it doesn't go that smoothly? What if there is no Will, no Executor of the Estate, what do you do? You call a Probate lawyer for one. Pay his/her fee and let them sort out the rest. You'll need to select an individual to act on everyone's behalf. Have documents notarized and returned to the lawyer. I've included: 'A What To Do List,' when a loved one dies. See the check list at the end of the book. The most frustrating thing during this process for me was waiting on individuals to have their waivers notarized, signed and returned. It took way too long for my family to get it together. But it's finally complete.

What Should The Family Do?

The family as a whole should keep the lines of communication open. Whether it be from visits, phone calls, text messages or video messaging. Because eventually friends, are going to stop calling as frequently or stopping by as life goes on. If the person who passed happens to have been The Rock of the family; The Glue that held it all together, someone else has to pick up the slack; it may take two of you to do it, but you have to keep in touch with each other. It doesn't have to be a daily call unless your family is just that close, and you speak daily anyway. But make a point to at least text once a week. Check on your family members. I try to make sure I do that with my brothers; if I don't text them, they usually text me. Also, keep yourself busy. Work, school, sporting events, social clubs, movies, concerts, reading, traveling; whatever you have to do to keep your mind on other things. That's not saying that you won't think of your loved one, but you won't dwell on their absence and be consumed with it. This could be your therapy. My therapy is writing this book, and along with that I visit my Mom's gravesite everyday I'm at work on my lunch break. That's what helps me. And knowing that the God I serve is My Prince of Peace. I've spoken with people who have lost loved ones, and feel that all they have to do is praise their way out of it. I can't disagree with that, because I know that all things are possible through Christ who strengthens me. There is no 'but,' but, I also know that depression is real. So is mental illness; we don't want to deal with it either. We make excuses for them, instead of seeking help. Don't try to get through this alone, if you know you can't handle it. You must take action and don't get stuck. You are not alone in this grieving process.

Coping With The Thought Of

Before September 9, 2016 a friend of mine was coping with the thought of losing her mother, and her father losing his wife of 60 years. Her mother had been battling cancer for a while and was now being put into hospice care. She called me Saturday September 10th to tell me happy Birthday. I said thank you, and then informed her that I lost Mom on yesterday (Friday). She was shocked, because Mom hadn't been sick. We continued to call and check on each other periodically, just to see how the other is doing. She as do I have our good days and not so good days.

Everyone grieves differently and on different levels. Some turn to the Lord, while others choose to keep it all inside. While yet others lash out at everyone who's in striking distance.

I can remember my mom telling me about a cousin whose mother died, and he died with her. Not in the physical sense, but emotionally. He stopped taking care of himself, wouldn't groom himself or even go outside of the house. This is an unhealthy way to deal with grief. Find someone to talk with. I can't reiterate it enough. If you can't talk, write. You are not alone when it comes to grief; we all grieve. It may be caused from a loved one's death, a person you were in a relationship with walks out or it could be over a pet dying. Whichever you are grieving over, seek counseling.

"What you are going to is greater than what you are going through." ~Pastor Tim Dixon

CONCLUSION

In conclusion, grief isn't easy and this book is solely designed so that you know that you are not alone. Someone else understands what you may be feeling right now or may have felt while you were grieving. Don't think that what you are feeling, thinking or how you may be acting during the grieving process is unusual. Everyone grieves differently. The most important part is that you grieve, and that you don't grieve in a way that is harmful to you, your health or to the ones around you.

Secondly, go through the process. It is a process to grieving. There are actually five steps to grieving. The first step is Denial where we don't want to accept the loss. Anger is the second step, we lash out at others and place blame either on them or ourselves. Bargaining is step three, Saying things like "I'd trade places with them, or I'd give anything." Fourth step is Depression, a feeling of hopelessness. And the Final step is Acceptance, where you accept it and are able to move on with your life. You don't get over the death of your loved one overnight. It will take time, patience and maybe a professional to help you through the process. But you can get through this.

My therapy is that I'm able to visit with my Mom and Stepdad every day on my lunch break. The Cemetery is on my route. I told my Mom I'll come every day until I don't have to anymore. And sometimes I don't have to go every day. I can skip days now. It helps to have an outlet. I found mine, you'll find yours too.

Third, talk to someone about how you are feeling. Find someone who is understanding, has been in your shoes and will help walk you through the grief process.

Finally, there will be times that you will still need encouragement, months after the initial death of your loved one. Sadness, loneliness or melancholy feelings will come during holidays, the anniversary of your loved ones' passing, birthdays, wedding anniversaries, a commercial or song. Feel free to follow me on Twitter and Instagram for encouragement to help you get through the grieving process one day at time. And just so you know, grieving for the loss of a loved one doesn't just have to be about a human, it could be an animal as well. And boy do I have stories for you about some pets that I've lost. But, we'll save that for next time.

What To Do When A Loved One Dies A Survivor's Checklist.

IMMEDIATELY FOLLOWING THE DEATH, YOU SHOULD:

- ☐ 1. Contact the funeral home to take your loved one into their care.
- ☐ 2. Contact your minister.
- ☐ 3. Alert immediate family members and close friends.
- ☐ 4. If employed, contact the deceased's employer.
- ☐ 5. If applicable, notify agent under Power of Attorney.
- ☐ 6. Alert the executor of your loved one's Will.
- ☐ 7. Notify religious, fraternal, and civic organizations that your loved one was a member of.
- ☐ 8. Notify your attorney regarding the

probate of the estate.

- ☐ 9. Arrange for the care of any dependents.
- ☐ 10. If the deceased had any pets, arrange for their immediate care.
- ☐ 11. Remove any valuables from the deceased's home, secure the residence, and take steps to make the home appear to be occupied (for example, use of lamp timers).
- ☐ 12. Arrange for the disposal of any perishables left in the deceased's home- such as food, refrigerated items, and existing refuse.
- ☐ 13. Alert the Post Office to forward the deceased's mail.

- ☐ 14. Locate loved one's important documents:

  - ☐ Will

  - ☐ Birth certificate

Grief Ministry

- ☐ Social Security card

- ☐ Marriage license

- ☐ Military discharge papers (DD-214)

- ☐ Deed to burial property

- ☐ Copy of funeral prearrangements

- ☐ Life insurance policies

☐ 15. Compile the following information that the funeral home will need in order to finalize the death certificate:

- ☐ Deceased's first, middle, and last name

- ☐ Deceased's Maiden Name (if applicable)

☐ Deceased's Home Address

☐ Deceased's Social Security Number

☐ Deceased's Date of Birth

☐ Deceased's Date of Death

☐ Deceased's Age

☐ Deceased's Gender

☐ Race/Ethnicity

☐ Marital Status

☐ Spouse's first and last name

☐ Deceased's highest level of education attained

Grief Ministry

- ☐ Deceased's Occupation

- ☐ Deceased's Place of Birth (City and State)

Deceased's Father's Name

- ☐ Birth City
- ☐ Birth State

Deceased's Mother's Name

- ☐ Birth City
- ☐ Birth State

If your loved one was a Veteran:

- ☐ Entered Service Date

- ☐ Entered Service Place

- ☐ Service Number

- ☐ Separated from Service Date

- ☐ Separated from Service Place

- ☐ Grade, Rank or Rating

- ☐ Organization and Branch of Service

WITHIN ONE MONTH OF THE DEATH, YOU SHOULD:

- ☐ 1. Consult with an attorney about probate.
- ☐ 2. Meet with an accountant to discuss estate taxes.
- ☐ 3. File claims with life insurance companies.
- ☐ 4. Contact the Social Security Administration and other government offices that may have been making payments to the decedent. If the decedent was your spouse, inquire about your eligibility for new benefits.
- ☐ 5. Notify the Registrar of Voters.
- ☐ 6. If the deceased's home is unoccupied, cancel unnecessary home services, such as newspaper delivery, cable service, etc.
- ☐ 7. Cancel deceased's prescriptions.
- ☐ 8. Contact the Department of Motor Vehicles to cancel deceased's driver's license and transfer titles of all registered

vehicles.

- [ ] 9. If your loved one was a veteran, inquire about benefits that you may be entitled to through the VA.
- [ ] 10. Contact the deceased's employer. Inquire about any 401 (k), pension, or company benefits that the decedent may be entitled to.
- [ ] 11. Notify all 3 credit reporting agencies.
- [ ] 12. Obtain a current copy of the deceased's credit report.
- [ ] 13. If the death was accidental, verify whether benefits are available on existing insurance policies.
- [ ] 14. Check for any life insurance benefits available through existing credit card or loan accounts.
- [ ] 15. File any outstanding claims for health insurance or Medicare
- [ ] 16. Obtain copies of deceased's outstanding bills

- [ ] 17. Locate and/or obtain other important paperwork of the necessary for the settlement of their estate:
    - [ ] At least 12 copies of the certified Death Certificates
    - [ ] Real estate deeds and titles
    - [ ] Stock certificates
    - [ ] Real estate titles
    - [ ] Loan paperwork
    - [ ] Bank and retirement account statements
    - [ ] Last 4 years of tax returns
- [ ] 18. Advise all creditors in writing that a death has occurred.

- ☐ 19. Change ownership of assets and lines of credit.
- ☐ 20. Update your Will.
- ☐ 21. Update beneficiaries on your life insurance policies, if necessary.
- ☐ 22. Send acknowledgement cards for flowers, donations, food and kindness. Also remember to thank pallbearers.
- ☐ 23. Organize and distribute decedent's personal belongings.
- ☐ 24. Remove loved one from marketing and mailing lists.

Grief Ministry

IMPORTANT CONTACT INFORMATION

DEPARTMENT OF VETERAN'S AFFAIRS

1-800-827-1000

www.vba.va.gov/VBA

SOCIAL SECURITY ADMINISTRATION

1-800-772-1213

www.ssa.gov/pgm/links_survivor.htm

CREDIT REPORTING AGENCIES

EQUIFAX

1-800-685-1111 • www.Equifax.com

TRANS UNION

1-800-888-4213 • www.TransUnion.com

EXPERIAN

1-888-397-3742 • www.Experain.com

[1]Special Thank You to Dennett, Craig and Pate for providing this checklist and for more information about them and if you need their services, contact: http://www.dcpate.com/

---

[1] Thank You to Dennett, Craig and Pate

Grief Ministry

Bible Verses To Help You Through

I have listed a few verses for Comfort and Inspiration. Knowing that Jesus is with me, comforts me at all times. I hope and pray, you find comfort in these verses.

Cling to the Lord and He will comfort you through the process of grieving and, in the future, will replace your sorrow with great, unending joy!

> Psalm 9:9 New International Version (NIV)
> 9 The Lord is a refuge for the oppressed,
> a stronghold in times of trouble.
>
> Psalm 30:2 New International Version (NIV)
> 2 Lord my God, I called to you for help,
> and you healed me.
>
> Psalm 46:1 New International Version (NIV)
> Psalm 46[a] For the director of music. Of the Sons of Korah. According to alamoth.[b] A song.
> 1 God is our refuge and strength, an ever-present help in trouble.
>
> Luke 6:21 New International Version (NIV)
> 21 Blessed are you who hunger now, for you will be satisfied. Blessed are you who weep now, for you will laugh.

Yvette J. Fleming

Isaiah 57:1-2 New International Version (NIV)
57 The righteous perish, and no one takes it to heart; the devout are taken away, and no one understands that the righteous are taken away to be spared from evil.
2 Those who walk uprightly enter into peace; they find rest as they lie in death.

Grief Ministry

"He is despised and rejected by men, a Man of sorrows and acquainted with grief" (Isaiah 53:4). Jesus, the greatest empathizer, understands what you are going through and will stay beside you.

"Blessed are those who mourn, for they shall be comforted" (Matthew 5:4). The Lord will wrap His arms of love and comfort around those who trust in Him.

"He heals the brokenhearted and binds up their wounds" (Psalm 147:3). Lean on God and allow Him to continue the process of healing your broken heart.

_____
_____
_____
_____
_____
_____
_____
_____
_____
_____
_____
_____
_____
_____
_____
_____
_____
_____
_____
_____
_____
_____
_____
_____
_____
_____

"Blessed be the God and Father of our Lord Jesus Christ, the Father of mercies and God of all comfort, who comforts us in all our tribulation, that we may be able to comfort those who are in any trouble" (2 Corinthians 1:3)

Grief Ministry

Comforting you is God's specialty. Being comforted can also mean receiving strength, encouragement and hope to deal with our trouble.

"Fear not, for I am with you; be not dismayed, for I am your God. I will strengthen you, yes, I will help you, I will uphold you with My righteous right hand" (Isaiah 41:10).

Grief Ministry

God promises to be with you and get you through this time of intense disappointment and loneliness.

"Yea, though I walk through the valley of the shadow of death, I will fear no evil; for You are with me; Your rod and Your staff, they comfort me" (Psalm 23:4).

Depend on His guidance to lead you out of that dark valley.

"I do not want you to be ignorant, brethren, concerning those who have fallen asleep, lest you sorrow as others who have no hope. For if we believe that Jesus died and rose again, even so God will bring with Him those who sleep in Jesus" (1 Thessalonians 4:13, 14).

As believers, we have hope of the resurrection promised by God.

Yvette J. Fleming

"The trumpet will sound, and the dead will be raised incorruptible, and we shall be changed. ... So when this corruptible has put on incorruption, and this mortal has put on immortality, then shall be brought to pass the saying that is written: 'Death is swallowed up in victory' " (1 Corinthians 15:52, 54).

At Christ's return, those who belong to Him will be raised and given life that will never end.

"God will wipe away every tear from their eyes; there shall be no more death, nor sorrow, nor crying. There shall be no more pain, for the former things have passed away" (Revelation 21:4). In the New Earth that God has promised to create, He will permanently dry your tears.

www.ingramcontent.com/pod-product-compliance
Lightning Source LLC
Chambersburg PA
CBHW071226160426
43196CB00012B/2425